2022
New Orleans

Restaurants

The Food Enthusiast's Long Weekend Guide

Andrew Delaplaine

Andrew Delaplaine is the Food Enthusiast.
When he's not playing tennis,
he dines anonymously
at the Publisher's (considerable) expense.

James Cubby – Senior Editor

The Food Enthusiast's
Long Weekend Guide

Table of Contents

INTRODUCTION

Only because it's one of the most fascinating cities in America, that's why.

In all my years of travel, I've always maintained that there are only a handful of cities in the U.S. that are thoroughly unique.

Of course, every place is unique *technically,* but what I mean by that is you'd be hard pressed to tell me the difference between Florence, S.C., and Darlington, S.C., if you were to drive through them. Or for that matter Sumter, S.C. Though they're different from each other, they're not *substantially* different. They're Podunk little towns in South

Carolina that have nothing to distinguish them except the road that luckily leads you out of them to some more interesting place. (I know. I lived in a town like that when I was a kid. Never again.)

New Orleans is not a town you can say that about.

With its rich cultural diversity (going back to the 1600s) that mixes in the French, the African, the Creole, the Spanish—and a lot of other influences—New Orleans is a fragrant stew of Life.

This is the birthplace of Jazz, which dates back to around 1910. I've always found it puzzling why Jazz is so unknown to younger audiences. It's such an American institution, but it doesn't seem to have found its place among the younger audiences today.

Since Katrina, there have been lots of great new restaurants that have opened, giving the city a food scene that rivals in richness what famous Southern chefs are doing in places like Charleston and Savannah.

And while you're sure to head straight to the French Quarter if this is your first visit, be sure to explore the Garden District if just to see the fabulous houses. You'll wish you lived in one of them.

Next to the French Quarter is the Central Business District (CBD) where the Superdome is located along with lots of museums.

Crime has gone up since Katrina, so you want to beware of certain areas. Ask your hotel or host if you have any questions. Most tourist areas are safe, however. Beware of hustles and pickpockets.

Also, there's a local saying, "Nothing good happens in the Quarter after midnight," and it's true. The bouncers and other security personnel in the clubs can be really nasty when dealing with drunks, and many have been sent to the hospital. Do not argue with them. You will not win.

Even with all my warnings, don't let me give you the impression you should think twice about coming here. You'd be *crazy* not to visit New Orleans if you have the chance. Arriving here always sends your senses into overdrive, into a fever pitch, whether it's your first time here or your tenth or thirtieth.

The uncomfortable muggy summer is the season that for me evokes the true sense of New Orleans. There's something about the town that makes you feel "air conditioning" is wrong. (Although it's a blessed relief to have it—I'm just talking metaphorically.) You wonder how people ever lived in the vortex of sweat and the smell of rotting tropical plants.

Those smells.

The humidity.

The jasmine.

The wrought iron grilles adorning the houses.

The smell of fried seafood.

The different dialects.

The St. Charles Avenue streetcar, still un-air-conditioned after all these years with its open windows and wooden benches.

The cemeteries that are more eerie than any others.

The music, the music, the music.

The rich Uptown lawyers taking their time over 4-hour lunches at Galatoire's while they swill down French burgundy and eat oysters Rockefeller.

The serenity of the Garden District.

The craziness of the Quarter.

It's all just too much. And all too wonderful.

How to say it: Don't use "Nawlins." The best way for an out-of-towner to say it is: *noo-OHR-luhnz*.

GETTING ABOUT

If you're confining your visit to the French Quarter and the CBD, a car will be more of a hassle than help. You can walk most everywhere, and for slightly longer jaunts, rely on the excellent trolley cars, buses and taxis to get around.

Tourist Information: www.neworleansonline.com

The A to Z Listings

Ridiculously Extravagant
Sensible Alternatives
Quality Bargain Spots

1000 FIGS
3141 Ponce de Leon St., 504-301-0848
https://www.1000figs.com/
CUISINE: Falafel / Middle Eastern
DRINKS: No Booze
SERVING: Lunch & Dinner; Closed Sundays

PRICE RANGE: $$
NEIGHBORHOOD: Mid-City
Small eatery with bleached wooden floors, spare wooden tables and mismatching wooden chairs make you think WOOD. The place is softened by some strategically placed plants perched on some shelves and these little plant-like tendrils hanging from the light fixtures. None of this matters, however, because the place is very popular, so be prepared to wait at peak times. Order from the counter and take a number so the server can find you. Sit at one of the few tables out front if you can snag one. Favorites: Lamb & Pork Kofta Kebab; Mint Adjika Braised Lamb Platter; Falafel Platter. Great for sharing.

ACME OYSTER HOUSE
724 Iberville St, New Orleans, 504-522-5973
www.acmeoyster.com
CUISINE: Seafood
DRINKS: Full Bar

SERVING: Lunch, Dinner
PRICE RANGE: $$
NEIGHBORHOOD: French Quarter
For more than 100 years this New Orleans eatery has been offering up delicious seafood dishes. Menu favorites include the fresh, hand-shucked oysters and Seafood Gumbo. There's often a wait for tables but it's worth it just to see the shuckers do their thing. On a stage this would be called performance art.

Veggie sampler at Addis Nola

ADDIS NOLA
422 S Broad St, New Orleans, 504-218-5321
https://www.addisnola.com/
CUISINE: Ethiopian / Comfort Food
DRINKS: Beer & Wine
SERVING: Lunch & Dinner
PRICE RANGE: $$
NEIGHBORHOOD: Tulane / Gravier
Not just new, but one of only two Ethiopian restaurants in Louisiana. Offering a menu of authentic Ethiopian cuisine, like Inerja, a popular flatbread. The

sides are excellent and flavorful—cabbage with carrots, yellow split peas, red lentils. My Favorites: Spicy Beef Ribs and Veggie Combo. Vegetarian offerings.

ANCORA PIZZERIA
4508 Freret St, New Orleans, 504-324-1636
www.ancorapizza.com
CUISINE: Pizza
DRINKS: Full Bar
SERVING: Dinner
PRICE RANGE: $$
NEIGHBORHOOD: Uptown/Freret
This pizzeria serves authentic Neapolitan pizzas and house-made salumi. The *arancini* (Sicilian fried rice balls coated with breadcrumbs) is wildly good. They also offer a great selection of Italian wines and hand-crafted cocktails. Closed Sundays.

ARNAUD'S
813 Bienville Ave, New Orleans, 504-523-5433
www.arnaudsrestaurant.com

CUISINE: Cajun/Creole
DRINKS: Full Bar
SERVING: Dinner
PRICE RANGE: $$$
NEIGHBORHOOD: French Quarter
Located just off Bourbon Street, this legendary eatery is the picture image of what you think of when you think of New Orleans, with its tile floor and the wrought iron porches. They serve classic Creole cuisine in an elegant atmosphere. The main dining room offers the perfect setting for romantic dinner and guests can enjoy live Dixieland Jazz in the **Jazz Bistro**. Menu favorites include: Rainbow Trout with Creole Sauce and Arnaud's Crab Cakes.

ATCHAFALAYA
901 Louisiana Ave, New Orleans, 504-891-9626
www.atchafalayarestaurant.com
CUISINE: Cajun/Creole
DRINKS: Full Bar
SERVING: Dinner nightly, Lunch daily except Tues & Wed
PRICE RANGE: $$
NEIGHBORHOOD: East Riverside
Some come for the build your own Bloody Mary bar. However, it's the food that keeps them coming back. Menu favorites include: Fried Chicken N Biscuits, eggs "treme" (they use crawfish in this dish) and Shrimp & Grits. Save room for the Blue Cheese Flan made with reduced balsamic and pumpkin seed brittle.

AUGUST
301 Tchoupitoulas St, New Orleans, 504-299-9777
www.restaurantaugust.com
CUISINE: French / Creole
DRINKS: Full Bar
SERVING: Dinner nightly; Lunch on Friday
PRICE RANGE: $$$$
NEIGHBORHOOD: Central Business District
Chef John Besh offers a creative menu of French cuisine in a beautifully decorated 19th century space. Striking chandeliers hang from high ceilings in this charming eatery. Brick walls are buttressed by ornate columns, giving the place an air of authority. Menu favorites include: Smoke swordfish cru and Crispy branzino with royal red shrimp. Or one of my favorites, the chili-enhanced soft shell crab. Reservations recommended.

BAKERY BAR
1179 Annunciation St, New Orleans, 504-210-8519
www.bakery.bar
CUISINE: Desserts
DRINKS: Full Bar
SERVING: Lunch, Dinner
PRICE RANGE: $$
NEIGHBORHOOD: Lower Garden District
Unique neighborhood spot with a bakery inspired menu and craft cocktails. Everything from cookies to cakes and cheese and charcuterie boards. There's a local favorite—the 7-layer "doberge" cake, with multiple flavors like cinnamon and chocolate. Board gamers paradise.

BARROW'S CATFISH
8300 Earhart Blvd #103, New Orleans, 504-265-8995
https://www.barrowscatfish.com/
CUISINE: Seafood
DRINKS: No Booze
SERVING: Lunch & Dinner, Closed Sun
PRICE RANGE: $$$
NEIGHBORHOOD: Gert Town
Serving excellent seafood cuisine since 1943, their menu has a definite Creole twist. Rough brick walls give the place a rustic feel. The biggest seller is their catfish, for which they are rightly famous worldwide. It's just lighted covered with cornmeal before it's flash fried and served hot. Melts in your mouth. My Other Favorites: Chargrilled Oysters (so tasty); Fried

shrimp that is so light and tender; an excellent Gumbo. Try the Bananas Foster Cake for dessert.

BEVI SEAFOOD CO

236 Carrollton Ave, New Orleans, 504-488-7503

www.beviseafoodco.com

CUISINE: Seafood/Sandwiches

DRINKS: Full bar

SERVING: Lunch & Dinner – Tues – Sat; Lunch only Sun & Mon

PRICE RANGE: $$

NEIGHBORHOOD: Mid-City

Market and restaurant in simple surroundings. Menu offers fresh fish, oysters and excellent po'boys. Try their combo – high po-boy and cup of soup. Or go for the Peacemaker, a big po'boy that includes Louisiana fried shrimp, roast beef & Swiss cheese.

THE BON TON CAFÉ

401 Magazine St, New Orleans, 504-524-3386

WEBSITE DOWN AT PRESSTIME

CUISINE: Cajun / Creole

DRINKS: Full Bar

SERVING: Lunch & Dinner; closed Sat & Sun

PRICE RANGE: $$$

NEIGHBORHOOD: Central Business District

Open since 1953, this quaint eatery offers a menu of classic Cajun dishes. Favorites include the Turtle soup, the shrimp and crab okra gumbo and the Crawfish Jambalaya. Get out your Crystal hot sauce. Save room for their delicious Bread pudding.

BRIGTSEN'S
723 Dante St, New Orleans, 504-861-7610
brigtsens.com
CUISINE: Cajun / Creole / Southern
DRINKS: Full Bar
SERVING: Dinner, Closed Sun & Mon
PRICE RANGE: $$$
NEIGHBORHOOD: Leonidas
Modern Creole eatery located in a quaint Victorian cottage. What the chef and his wife do here is quite remarkable: they merged (it's called "fusion" these days) Cajun cuisine from the countryside and bayou

wetlands with elements of Creole cuisine more commonly found in the city. From this unique perspective, they created such dishes as Rabbit Andouille Gumbo; the breaded and quickly fried rabbit is my absolute favorite; Pork Chops served with potato hash sweetened with tasso; Parmesan-crusted Gulf fish with a dollop of crab meat on top of it; Roasted Tripletail Amandine; BBQ Seasoned Redfish with Chipotle Grits Cake. The Southern-inspired desserts are just as novel as their main plates, so save some room for them. Reservations recommended.

BORGNE
601 Loyola Ave, New Orleans, 504-613-3860
www.borgnerestaurant.com
CUISINE: Seafood/American/Southern
DRINKS: Full Bar
SERVING: Lunch, Dinner
PRICE RANGE: $$$
NEIGHBORHOOD: Central Business District
This is a favorite destination for local seafood and Southern dishes. It's a very simple room, big and open and airy, and sends off the same vibe you get at the fish camps that you run across when traveling along the waterways. Menu favorites include: Louisiana White Shrimp Risotto, a spicy shrimp rémoulade, Stuffed Flounder and Sheepshead Fish in a Bag. The desserts are also worth trying like the Lime Ice Box Parfait and the Chocolate Hazelnut Puddin.

BOUCHERIE
8115 Jeannette St, New Orleans, 504-862-5514
www.boucherie-nola.com
CUISINE: Barbeque/Southern
DRINKS: Full Bar
SERVING: Lunch, Dinner
PRICE RANGE: $$
NEIGHBORHOOD: Uptown
One would never think that this Southern-flavored bistro began its life as a food truck. The menu is quite inventive with dishes like Boudin balls and Krispy Kreme bread pudding. Menu favorites include: Blackened shrimp with grit toast and Wagyu Beef Brisket.

BOULIGNY TAVERN
3641 Magazine St, New Orleans, 504-891-1810
www.boulignytavern.com

CUISINE: Tapas/Small Plates
DRINKS: Full Bar
SERVING: Dinner, Late night
PRICE RANGE: $$
NEIGHBORHOOD: East Riverside
This relaxed eatery is basically a gastropub that offers small-plate dining. Menu favorites include croquettes with chorizo and comte, gouda beignets and meatball flatbread. They also offer an impressive list of selected wines and a well-crafted cocktail menu with exotic drink specialties like the Sage Julep. Closed Sundays.

BOURBON HOUSE
144 Bourbon St, New Orleans, 504-522-0111
www.bourbonhouse.com
CUISINE: Cajun/Creole
DRINKS: Full Bar
SERVING: Lunch, Dinner
PRICE RANGE: $$$
NEIGHBORHOOD: French Quarter
Chef Dickie Brennan is well known in New Orleans and offers a menu of great Cajun/Creole cuisine. Menu favorites include: New Orleans Style BBQ Shrimp and Redfish on the Half Shell, though I'm especially fond of the oysters with caviar and Parmesan. This is truly a fine dining experience. And for the bourbon, this place offers an impressive selection of small batch and single barrel bourbons. If you're a bourbon fan, you must try the Frozen Bourbon Milk Punch—it's basically a milkshake, but one you won't soon forget.

BRENNAN'S
417 Royal St, 504-525-9711
https://www.brennansneworleans.com/
CUISINE: Cajun/Creole
DRINKS: Full Bar
SERVING: Breakfast, Lunch, & Dinner
PRICE RANGE: $$$
NEIGHBORHOOD: French Quarter
Most fine dining places aren't open for breakfast, but this one is. This upscale establishment located in a distinctive pinkish 2-level building has been known (since they opened in 1946) for its hearty Creole cuisine. Everybody remembers the lively murals in its main dining room. In good weather, there's a nice courtyard where you can lunch or dine. (Really pretty at night, magical.) Observe the turtles sunbathing on rocks in the little pool. (They don't use those turtles for the Turtle Soup they serve inside, or I hope they don't.) Great spot for breakfast (get the eggs Sardou, with artichokes & poached eggs smothered in Hollandaise). Favorites: BBQ Shrimp Quenelles; Blackened Redfish; Rabbit (crispy skin); Garlic Prawns. Bananas Foster dessert (which was invented here) is a must, and it's prepared tableside, the way it's supposed to be. Reservations recommended. Delicious fresh juices.

BROUSSARD'S
819 Conti St, New Orleans, 504-581-3866
www.broussards.com
CUISINE: Seafood, French, and Cajun/Creole
DRINKS: Full Bar
SERVING: Lunch, Dinner
PRICE RANGE: $$$
NEIGHBORHOOD: French Quarter
A New Orleans fixture for nearly a century, Broussard's offers a menu that mixes French and Creole influences. Here you'll get a dining experience that you won't forget. Menu favorites include: Oven Baked Dover Sole and Gulf Shrimp Lean Lafitte. Desserts are tasty too with selections like Crepes Broussard and the Bananas Foster.

BYWATER AMERICAN BISTRO
2900 Chartres St, 504-605-3827
http://bywateramericanbistro.com/

CUISINE: American (New)
DRINKS: Full Bar
SERVING: Dinner, Brunch on Sat & Sun, Closed on Mon & Tues.
PRICE RANGE: $$
NEIGHBORHOOD: Bywater
Busy eatery where you can see into the open kitchen from your seat at the bar to watch the cooks toiling away under a row of big gleaming copper pots dangling from the ceiling. Old brick walls with wood accents. A chest-high divider separates the bar from the dining room. This is a popular Brunch destination. Favorites: Jerk Chicken Rice; Crispy Hogs Head Boudin; Chicken liver parfait; Rabbit Curry; Kimchi fried rice; Hot Sausage, Egg & Cheese Sandwich (brunch only). Reservations recommended. Small cocktail menu is worthy a second look.

CAFÉ SBISA
1011 Decatur St, New Orleans, 504-522-5565
www.cafesbisanola.com
CUISINE: Southern/Seafood
DRINKS: Full Bar
SERVING: Dinner, Lunch on Sun; Closed Mon & Tues
PRICE RANGE: $$
NEIGHBORHOOD: French Quarter
Ornately decorated venue offering classic (and expertly prepared) French-Creole cuisine since 1899. They had lots of damage during Hurricane Katrina, but recovered eventually. Check out the daily gumbos—they're great whatever the day happens to

be. Favorites: Turtle soup and Louisiana Blue Crab Cakes. Nice wine selection.

CANE & TABLE
1113 Decatur St, New Orleans, 504-581-1112
www.caneandtablenola.com
CUISINE: Caribbean
DRINKS: Full Bar
SERVING: Dinner
PRICE RANGE: $$
NEIGHBORHOOD: French Quarter
This eatery has an old-world ambience (what you might imagine a Colonial-era pub or inn might feel like) with a menu of primarily small plates. Favorites include their delicious ribs soaked in El Dorado rum, braised in ginger, garlic, peppers. The ribs are then battered and deep-fried, which gives you a crispy shell surrounding the succulent meat. The craft cocktails emphasize good aged rums and employ house-made syrups to finish them off perfectly.

CASAMENTO'S
4330 Magazine St, New Orleans, 504-895-9761
www.casamentosrestaurant.com
CUISINE: Seafood
DRINKS: Full Bar
SERVING: Lunch daily, Dinner Thurs. – Sat; closed Sun
PRICE RANGE: $$
NEIGHBORHOOD: East Riverside
Cut little seafood eatery, open since 1919, that's a little off the beaten path but worth the search. Cash-

only spot serves fresh oysters & other seafood in a compact, mosaic-tiled space.

CHARLIE'S STEAK HOUSE
4510 Dryades St, New Orleans, 504-895-9323
https://charliessteakhousenola.com/
CUISINE: Steakhouse
DRINKS: Full Bar
SERVING: Dinner, Closed Sun & Mon
PRICE RANGE: $$$
NEIGHBORHOOD: Uptown
Since 1932, this old-fashioned steakhouse has been serving thick-cut steaks and classic sides. Popular with locals. Forget all about Smith & Wollensky, Del Frisco's, Peter Lugar, the Palm or Ruth's Chris—those famous steakhouses with the tufted leather booths, the dark paneling, the air of mega-deals being made in hushed whispers. No, this is strictly a working class steakhouse. From the outside it looks like a beat-up old pool hall. Inside, it doesn't look much different. But no pool hall ever had food like

this. My Favorites: NY Strip and a Large T-Bone that weighs in at 32 oz. I always get the Crabmeat au Gratin to share with someone. So yummy. Impressive wine list. Reservations recommended.

COCHON BUTCHER

930 Tchoupitoulas St, New Orleans, 504-588-7675
www.cochonbutcher.com
CUISINE: Sandwiches
DRINKS: Full Bar
SERVING: Lunch, Dinner
PRICE RANGE: $$
NEIGHBORHOOD: Central Business District
No-frills butcher shop offering a great selection of sandwiches, with an emphasis on the muffuletta, which they serve hot unless you order it cold. The chef has a special oven to heat them, using a combination of steam and heat that melts the cheese to highlight the flavors of the meat. Try the Le Pig Mac – their version of the Big Mac and the Duck Pastrami Slider. Butcher counter with selection of meats. Le Pig Mac, the mac and cheese and blueberry cheesecake. Menu favorites include: Buckboard Bacon Melt and Roasted Turkey with Arugula, Tomato and Fontina. The butcher shop offers in-house made meats, terrines, sausages, and fresh cut meats. Great place for catering needs. No reservations.

COMMANDER'S PALACE
1403 Washington Ave, New Orleans, 504-899-8221
www.commanderspalace.com
CUISINE: Cajun/Creole
DRINKS: Full Bar
SERVING: Lunch, Dinner
PRICE RANGE: $$$$
NEIGHBORHOOD: Garden District
This place gets as much hype as a tourist trap but there's a difference: this is the "Real Thing." In a classic Victorian setting, this eatery offers a menu that combines modern New Orleans cooking with Haute Creole. This is the place decades ago where French Creole and Cajun were first blended with nouvelle cuisine. There have been many copycats, and many of them are very good, but this place still sets a very high bar. Though the place can be quite expensive, one tip followed frequently by locals is to

head here for lunch on weekdays when it's always very cheap. Menu favorites include: Pecan Crusted Gulf Fish, Absinthe Poached Oysters, Turtle Soup (spiked with sherry) and Cast Iron Seared Foie Gras. You can't leave without trying the bread pudding soufflé. The bar offers a creative cocktail menu with selections like the Vieux Carre Cocktail. The white-glove service is impeccable.

THE COMPANY BURGER
4600 Freret St, New Orleans, 504-267-0320
www.thecompanyburger.com
CUISINE: Burgers/Fast Food
DRINKS: Full Bar
SERVING: Lunch, Dinner
PRICE RANGE: $$
NEIGHBORHOOD: Uptown
As the name suggests, this place specializes in burgers of the thin patty type cooked on a griddle. They are really juicy and tasty. They have a selection of great burgers served with homemade condiments.

There's also the "Curewich," nicknamed for the nearby bar **CURE**, because so many of the staff order it: it's a grilled cheese with bacon and egg. The owner's mother bakes the delicious desserts.

COMPERE LAPIN
535 Tchoupitoulas St, New Orleans, 504-599-2119
www.comperelapin.com
CUISINE: American/Caribbean
DRINKS: Full Bar
SERVING: Lunch & Dinner
PRICE RANGE: $$$
NEIGHBORHOOD: Warehouse District
Located in The Old No. 77 Hotel & Chandlery, Chef/Owner Nina Compton's menu features a combination of Caribbean, French, and Italian influences. (She's from St. Lucia and her grandmother was British.) Menu favorites include: Curried Goat and Broiled Shrimp.

THE COUNTRY CLUB
634 Louisa St, New Orleans, 504-945-0742
www.thecountryclubneworleans.com
CUISINE: American/Southern
DRINKS: Full Bar
SERVING: Lunch, Dinner
PRICE RANGE: $$
NEIGHBORHOOD: Bywater
This Country Club offers a party atmosphere with a clothing optional pool and hot tub but some people go just for the delicious food. Chef Maryjane Rosas offers a menu with a variety of treats from chicken and waffles to BBQ delicacies. Menu favorites include: Honey Lamb Roast and Seared Trout with Roasted Kohlrabi. This is also a popular Brunch destination.

COURT OF TWO SISTERS
613 Royal St, New Orleans, 504-522-7261
www.courtoftwosisters.com
CUISINE: American/Southern
DRINKS: Full Bar
SERVING: Breakfast, Lunch, Dinner
PRICE RANGE: $$$
NEIGHBORHOOD: French Quarter
This venerable establishment dates back to 1832. What you want to experience here is the courtyard with its overflowing vines of wisteria creating a luscious canopy overhead. Crawfish omelets, Cajun past and Creole jambalaya are big dishes here. Their brunch consistently wins awards. A jazz band is usually working the crowd.

DAT DOG
5030 Rue Freret St, 504-899-6883
3336 Magazine St (Uptown), 504-324-2226
601 Frenchmen St (The Marigny), 504-309-3362
www.datdognola.com
CUISINE: Fast Food
DRINKS: Full Bar
SERVING: Lunch & Dinner
PRICE RANGE: $
Famous for their gourmet hot dogs (some made with crawfish and alligator) served with whatever you want on them on sourdough rolls. Toppings include guacamole, Andouille sauce, hummus, etc. Very creative hot dog menu.

THE DELACHAISE
3442 St. Charles Ave, New Orleans, 504-895-0858
www.thedelachaise.com
CUISINE: American
DRINKS: Full Bar
SERVING: Dinner
PRICE RANGE: $$
NEIGHBORHOOD: Central City/Uptown
This is a popular watering hole for preppies and hipsters who love the impressive selection of wine and beer. The menu includes favorites like Flank Steak Bruschetta and Moules et Frites. The food is really just a step up from bar fare but it's creative and tasty.

DIMARTINO'S
700 S. Tyler, Covington, 985-276-6460
www.dimartinos.com

CUISINE: Muffulettas
DRINKS: No Booze
SERVING: Lunch & Dinner
PRICE RANGE: $$
NEIGHBORHOOD: Covington
Popular eatery with counter-serve. Menu of muffulettas, po'boys, burgers, and Italian entrees. Favorites: their signature dish - DiMartino's Famous New Orleans Muffuletta and Grilled Chicken Italian Salad. Eat in or to go.

DOMENICA
123 Baronne St, New Orleans, 504-648-6020
www.domenicarestaurant.com
CUISINE: Italian/Tapas
DRINKS: Full Bar
SERVING: Lunch, Dinner
PRICE RANGE: $$
NEIGHBORHOOD: Central Business District
Located inside the Roosevelt Hotel, this John Besh restaurant offers delicious Italian fare. Menu favorites include: Roasted Carrot pizza and Rigatoni. Save room for the Gianduja Budino, a delicious dessert. You'll also find a menu of custom-brewed beers and Italian wines.

DOMILISE'S PO'BOY & BAR
5240 Annunciation St, New Orleans, 504-899-9126
www.domilisespoboys.com
CUISINE: Barbeque/Seafood
DRINKS: Beer & Wine Only
SERVING: Lunch & Dinner; closed Sun
PRICE RANGE: $$$

NEIGHBORHOOD: West Riverside; Uptown
Local counter-serve eatery offering up giant po'boys and beers makes this one of the highlights of your visit. Don't let the fact that the place needs a paint job deter you. When you get a look at the tiny kitchen here, you'll wonder how these guys turn out the wonderful food that they do in such quantities. While you can order the usual suspects when it comes to po'boys (fried oyster, fried shrimp and roast beef), I always opt for one of their other po'boys, like the cheeseburger po'boy or the smoked hot sausage. Their condiments (hot sauces, mustards, etc.) are better than average, far better.

DONG PHUONG BAKERY & RESTAURANT
14207 Chef Menteur Hwy, New Orleans, 504-254-0214
www.dpbakeshop.com
CUISINE: Vietnamese/Chinese
DRINKS: No Booze
SERVING: Lunch, Dinner
PRICE RANGE: $
NEIGHBORHOOD: East New Orleans
There are two sides to this place, the bakery side and the restaurant side. An amazing selection of baked goods and pastries on that side, while over in the restaurant, expect a large variety of Vietnamese dishes. There's quite a large Vietnamese population in NOLA, so I've listed some of the best spots. This one is good for take-out. The bakery provides breads to many local restaurants so you know it's good.

DRAGO'S SEAFOOD RESTAURANT
2 Poydras St, New Orleans, 504-584-3911
www.dragosrestaurant.com
CUISINE: Seafood
DRINKS: Full Bar
SERVING: Lunch, Dinner
PRICE RANGE: $$
NEIGHBORHOOD: Central Business District
This is a classic New Orleans seafood eatery with an impressive menu. Menu favorites include: Lobster and Shrimp & Grits. Many favor their classic oysters, and this would be a good place to savor a Crescent City specialty, **Charbroiled Oysters**, made with garlic, herbs and butter, topped with flaky parmesan and Romano cheese. The last time I was here, I easily consumed 2 dozen of these mouthwatering delicacies. There's also a gluten-free menu.

EAT
900 Dumaine St, New Orleans, 504-522-7222
www.eatnola.com

CUISINE: Creole/Cajun/Soul Food
DRINKS: No Booze
SERVING: Lunch & Dinner, weekend Brunch; closed Mon
PRICE RANGE: $$
NEIGHBORHOOD: French Quarter
This gay-operated hipster hangout is a cut above most French Quarter spots. They have updated takes on classic New Orleans dishes like BBQ shrimp, crawfish & red beans, smoked salmon atop deviled eggs. It's all in a charming brick and pale-blue dining room.

ELIZABETH'S
601 Gallier St, New Orleans, 504-944-9272
www.elizabethsrestaurantnola.com
CUISINE: Southern
DRINKS: Full Bar
SERVING: Breakfast, Lunch & Dinner; No Dinner on Sun
PRICE RANGE: $$
NEIGHBORHOOD: Bywater
This busy spot offers down-home country classics and great po' boys. Dishes are huge. Great spot for breakfast. (Order the French toast stuffed with bananas Foster, out of this world.)

EMERIL'S DELMONICO
1300 St Charles Ave, New Orleans, 504-525-4937
www.emerilsrestaurants.com
CUISINE: Cajun/Creole
DRINKS: Full Bar
SERVING: Dinner
PRICE RANGE: $$$
NEIGHBORHOOD: Mid-City; Lower Garden District

Located on the St. Charles Avenue streetcar line, this legendary eatery offers an impressive menu of Cajun and Creole dishes. Emeril pays special attention to his flagship restaurant and the menu changes 3 or 4 times a year, keeping it fresh and alive. Menu favorites include: Moulard Duck Breast and Beef & Pork Terrine. His version of the local favorite, "Dirty Rice," includes crispy pork cheek and scallions. Save room for dessert and order the Bananas Foster for two that's prepared at your table, you won't be disappointed.

GALATOIRE'S
209 Bourbon St, New Orleans, 504-525-2021
www.galatoires.com/home
CUISINE: French
DRINKS: Full Bar
SERVING: Lunch, Dinner
PRICE RANGE: $$$
NEIGHBORHOOD: French Quarter
This French eatery specializes in old-fashioned Creole cuisine. Menu favorites include: Duck Crepes and Trout Almandine Meuniere. It's a two-level restaurant with some of the upstairs rooms overlooking Bourbon Street. This place is busy but no reservations are accepted.

GAUTREAU'S
1728 Soniat St, New Orleans, 504-899-7397
www.gautreausrestaurant.com/
CUISINE: American (New) / French
DRINKS: Full Bar
SERVING: Dinner; closed Sun
PRICE RANGE: $$$
NEIGHBORHOOD: Uptown
A little secluded eatery that offers a menu of New American-French cuisine. Favorites include: Duck confit and Halibut, pork cheek with Korean chili glaze. Try their banana split – it's a winner.

GREEN GODDESS
307 Exchange Pl, New Orleans, 504-301-3347
www.greengoddessrestaurant.com
CUISINE: American/Vegetarian
DRINKS: Full Bar

SERVING: Lunch, Dinner
PRICE RANGE: $$
NEIGHBORHOOD: French Quarter
Here you'll find traditional New Orleans fare that has been influence by a variety of cultures. Menu dishes include French, Thai, Cajun and Soul. Menu also includes vegetarian and vegan options. The bar offers a creative cocktail menu and serves quality local and regional brews. Closed Monday & Tuesday.

GW FINS
808 Bienville, New Orleans, 504-581-3467
www.GWFins.com
CUISINE: Seafood
DRINKS: Full Bar
SERVING: Dinner
PRICE RANGE: $$$
NEIGHBORHOOD: French Quarter
Here you'll find the finest quality seafood from around the world. Menu favorites include: Whole

roasted Red Snapper and Blue Nose Bass from New Zealand. Try the Lobster Dumplings served with Fennel and Tomatoes and you'll be back for more. If there's room for dessert, try the individual homemade apple pie served warm and topped with vanilla ice cream. Their wine list is very impressive with more than 100 labels, most available by the glass.

GUY'S PO-BOYS
5259 Magazine St, New Orleans, 504-891-5025
No Website
CUISINE: Sandwiches/Cajun/Creole
DRINKS: No Booze
SERVING: Lunch; closed Sun
PRICE RANGE: $
NEIGHBORHOOD: West Riverside
Great place for lunch or a quick dinner. It's best to call ahead to order. Specialty – Po-boys. There are only about 15 seats so most people take their food to go. Get the grilled shrimp po'boy.

HERBSAINT
701 St Charles Ave, New Orleans, 504-524-4114
www.herbsaint.com/
CUISINE: French
DRINKS: Full Bar
SERVING: Lunch & Dinner weekdays, Dinner Sat; closed Sun
PRICE RANGE: $$$
NEIGHBORHOOD: Warehouse District
Located in a great spot with outdoor seating, this eatery offers an upscale menu of French and American cuisine. Favorites include: Louisiana

Shrimp with Rice, artichoke and Maitake and the Muscovy Duck Leg Confit, which comes with a Dirty Rice with delicious hints of citrus "gastrique." This dish has been on the menu forever, and I always get it. Delicious desserts like their Greek Yogurt Cheesecake with roasted peaches.

HIGH HAT CAFÉ
4500 Freret St, New Orleans, 504-754-1336
www.highhatcafe.com/
CUISINE: Southern
DRINKS: Full Bar
SERVING: Lunch, Dinner
PRICE RANGE: $$

NEIGHBORHOOD: Uptown
This casual neighborhood eatery offers a menu specializing in the classic food from the Mississippi Delta. Menu favorites include: Catfish (fried, of course—I don't think they could ever cook catfish any other way) and Smoked Roasted Chicken. The bar has a nice wine list and serves local draft beers and craft cocktails.

JAMILA'S TUNISIAN CAFÉ
7808 Maple St, New Orleans, 504-866-4366
http://www.jamilascafe.com/
CUISINE: Mediterranean / Tunisian

DRINKS: Beer & Wine
SERVING: Dinner, Closed Mon
PRICE RANGE: $$$
NEIGHBORHOOD: East Carrollton
Small Mediterranean eatery with a heavy Creole flair. Husband and wife team of Jamila (she cooks) and Moncef (he brags about her) create a welcoming atmosphere. My Favorites: Lamb kabobs; the incredible Lamb Sausage; Eggplant Salad; Crawfish Bisque. The couscous here is divine. Impressive wine list. Nice desserts. Family-friendly.

JOSEPHINE ESTELLE
ACE HOTEL
600 Carondelet St, 504-930-3070
http://josephineestelle.com/
https://www.acehotel.com/neworleans/
CUISINE: Italian
DRINKS: Full Bar
SERVING: Breakfast, Lunch, & Dinner
PRICE RANGE: $$
NEIGHBORHOOD: Warehouse District
Beautiful bistro-style eatery with stately columns supporting the high ceiling, this place also has a roomy bar area where I like to enjoy the Italian specialties they serve. Favorites: Waldorf Salad (you rarely see this on a menu, and this is a good rendition); Pasta with zucchini; Gemelli (octopus bolognese); Soft Shell Crab with peaches & mushrooms; and Farmer's Breakfast. Tempting dessert menu.

THE JOINT
701 Mazant St, New Orleans, 504-949-3232
www.alwayssmokin.com
CUISINE: BBQ/Southern
DRINKS: Full Bar
SERVING: Lunch & Dinner; closed Sunday
PRICE RANGE: $$
NEIGHBORHOOD: Bywater
A menu of real Western-style BBQ keeps this place packed. Great selections of pulled pork, beef brisket and chicken and ribs. If you've never tasted peanut butter pie, then you're in for a treat. (This pie turns my stomach but those who like it *rave* about the version to be found here.)

KILLER POBOYS
Erin Rose Bar
811 Conti St, New Orleans, 504-252-6745
www.killerpoboys.com
CUISINE: Sandwiches
DRINKS: Full bar

SERVING: Lunch & Dinner; closed Tues
PRICE RANGE: $$
NEIGHBORHOOD: French Quarter
Located in the back of the Erin Rose bar, this little spot sells a variety of po'boys. Favorite: Pork belly Po'boy with lime slaw. It's a real standout.

Inside at La Petite Grocery

LA PETITE GROCERY
4238 Magazine St, New Orleans, 504-891-3377
https://www.lapetitegrocery.com/
CUISINE: French Bistro
DRINKS: Full Bar
SERVING: Lunch & Dinner, Dinner only on Mon & Tues
PRICE RANGE: $$$
NEIGHBORHOOD: East Riverside

Housed in a cottage formerly a grocery store Uptown, hence the name. Here you'll find homemade Louisiana fare with a French twist. Favorites: Turtle Bolognese; Crab Beignets; Crispy Pork Belly and Steak Tartare. New Orleans inspired desserts like the Stuffed Coconut Snoball. Reservations recommended.

LENGUA MADRE
1245 Constance St, New Orleans, 504-655-1338
lenguamadrenola.com
CUISINE: Mexican
DRINKS: Full Bar
SERVING: Dinner, Closed Mon & Tues
PRICE RANGE: $$
NEIGHBORHOOD: Lower Garden District
Unique Mexican eatery offering a 5-course tasting and a la carte menus. Though a lot of prix-fixe

restaurants have a certain "air" about them, this one doesn't. Very comfortable surroundings. I always feel like I'm visiting a friend when I come here. You will, too. From the outside, it's a little rough looking, but inside is a lot snappier. My Favorites: Shrimp Reduction Amuse; the oh-so-flavorful Gulf shrimp bouillon; and Crab meat with Avocado Tostado. Wine pairing. Impressive Mexican Spirit list.

LIUZZA'S BY THE TRACK
1518 North Lopez, New Orleans, 504-218-7888
https://liuzzasbythetrack.com/
CUISINE: Cajun/Creole
DRINKS: Full Bar
SERVING: Lunch, Dinner
PRICE RANGE: $$
NEIGHBORHOOD: Mid-City

This eatery offers a New Orleans menu of Creole and Cajun with a little Italian. Menu favorites include: Shrimp, Corn & Okra Stew and Seafood Lasagna. Their po'boys are so tasty but also too large to finish. Closed Sundays.

LUCA EATS
7329 Cohn St, New Orleans, 504-866-1166
www.lucaeats.com
CUISINE: American (Traditional)
DRINKS: No Booze
SERVING: Breakfast & Lunch
PRICE RANGE: $$
NEIGHBORHOOD: Audubon
A rundown seedy little place that's nonetheless popular because it serves good food. Menu picks: Fried bell peppers & corn grits and Oreo Beignets. Try their delicious homemade chips.

LUVI
5236 Tchoupitoulas St, New Orleans, 504-605-3340
https://www.luvirestaurant.com/
CUISINE: Asian
DRINKS: Full Bar
SERVING: Dinner, Closed Sun & Mon
PRICE RANGE: $$
NEIGHBORHOOD: West Riverside
Small Asian eatery mixing Japanese and Chinese cuisines situated in a quaint cottage Uptown offering homestyle Shanghai cuisine with a twist. Favorites: Curried Dumplings and Tuna meatballs. Menu updated regularly. Reservations recommended.

MAGASIN VIETNAMESE CAFÉ
4201 Magazine St, New Orleans, 504-896-7611
No website
CUISINE: Vietnamese
DRINKS: No Booze
SERVING: Lunch, Dinner
PRICE RANGE: $$
NEIGHBORHOOD: East Riverside
This Vietnamese eater offers a variety of Pho. Menu favorites include the Filet Mignon Pho (but I like the Oxtail Pho better) and the Avocado Spring Roll. The pig belly is braised for 40 hours until it forms a thick sauce. A bare-bones eatery offering superior food.

MAHONY'S PO'BOYS & SEAFOOD
3454 Magazine St, New Orleans, 504-899-3374
www.mahonyspoboys.com
CUISINE: Cajun/Creole
DRINKS: Full Bar
SERVING: Lunch & Dinner
PRICE RANGE: $$$
NEIGHBORHOOD: East Riverside
This counter shop offers a great menu of sandwiches and po'boys and it's hard to beat this place. Two years in a row they won the Oak Street Po'boy Festival (Po'boy Preservation Festival) with a po'boy that included fried chicken livers and Creole coleslaw. The Peacemaker po'boy has fried oysters, bacon and cheddar cheese. (Feel the heart attack coming on?) Great jambalaya also, as well as fried green tomatoes with remoulade sauce. It gets busy, so don't be surprised if there's a wait.

MANNING'S
519 Fulton St, New Orleans, 504-593-8118
www.caesars.com/harrahs-new-orleans/restaurants
CUISINE: American/Sports Bar
DRINKS: Full Bar
SERVING: Lunch, Dinner
PRICE RANGE: $$
NEIGHBORHOOD: Central Business District
Located at Harrah Casino, this Sports Bar offers a menu of American favorites with some Creole classics. This is the perfect place for sports fans with more than 30 flat screen TVs and a mega-screen TV.

MANNY RANDAZZO KING CAKES
3515 N Hullen St, Metairie, 504-456-1476
www.randazzokingcake.com/
CUISINE: Bakery
DRINKS: No Booze
SERVING: 6:30 a.m. – 5 p.m.
PRICE RANGE: $$
NEIGHBORHOOD: Metairie

Bakery specializing in king cakes in a variety of flavors. Specialty cakes baked and delivered year round.

MARJIE'S GRILL

320 S Broad Ave, New Orleans, 504-603-2234
www.marjiesgrill.com
CUISINE: Southern/Asian Fusion
DRINKS: Full bar
SERVING: Lunch & Dinner; closed Sun
PRICE RANGE: $$
NEIGHBORHOOD: Tulane / Gravier / Mid-City
Casual eatery specializing in Southern Asian cuisine mixed creatively together with Gulf ingredients. Try an order of pig knuckles—salty and crispy, covered with cane syrup. There's a BBQ pit out back where a lot of the food is coal-roasted. Shrimp are coated with cornmeal before frying. Favorites: BBQ pork shoulder and Spice-rubbed Gulf fish. Happy hour 4-6 weeknights.

MAYPOP

611 O'Keefe St, New Orleans, 504-518-6345
www.maypopnola.com
CUISINE: American (New)/Dim Sum
DRINKS: Full Bar
SERVING: Lunch, Dinner
PRICE RANGE: $$
NEIGHBORHOOD: Warehouse District
Popular eatery offers a menu of Southern-Asian fusion mixed in with Creole specialties. Favorites:

House-cured meats and Red curry octopus pasta. Menu changes regularly.

MERIL
424 Girod St, New Orleans, 504-526-3745
www.emerilsrestaurants.com/meril
CUISINE: American (New)
DRINKS: Full Bar
SERVING: Lunch, Dinner
PRICE RANGE: $$
NEIGHBORHOOD: Warehouse District
Great local eatery named after owner Emeril Lagasse's daughter Meril is unlike his other spots in the city, more modern (reclaimed wood in the interior) and adventurous and allows for numerous international influences. Favorites: Fried blue crab; Buttermilk biscuit with foie gras & blackberry jam; Spanish croquettes with ham, manchego, & piquillo pepper sauce; and Korean fried chicken. Creative desserts like Banana foster cake with ice cream or the lemon ice box pie. The cocktail menu is similarly adventurous, and ingredients are top-notch. Try the classic Hemingway daiquiri, as I did.

MIMI'S IN THE MARIGNY
2600 Chartres St, New Orleans, 504-872-9868
www.mimismarigny.com
CUISINE: Tapas
DRINKS: Full Bar
SERVING: Dinner, Late night
PRICE RANGE: $$
NEIGHBORHOOD: Marigny
This great hipster dive serves a menu of tasty tapas. Menu favorites include: Goat Cheese Croquetas and Mushroom Manchego Toast. Live music.

MINT MODERN BISTRO & BAR
5100 Freret St, New Orleans, 504-218-5534
www.mintmodernbistro.com
WEBSITE DOWN AT PRESSTIME
CUISINE: Vietnamese
DRINKS: Full Bar
SERVING: Lunch & Dinner; closed Mon
PRICE RANGE: $$
NEIGHBORHOOD: Freret

A popular modern eatery offering up a menu of Vietnamese classics and other popular Asian dishes. Menu picks include: Vietnamese pork tacos and the Kim Chi Burger.

MOTHER'S RESTAURANT
401 Poydras St, New Orleans, 504-523-9656
www.mothersrestaurant.net/
CUISINE: Cajun/Creole, American (New), Soul Food, Southern
DRINKS: Beer & Wine Only
SERVING: Breakfast, Lunch & Dinner
PRICE RANGE: $$
NEIGHBORHOOD: Central Business District
This popular red-bricked cafeteria-style eatery has been dishing out Southern fare and delicious po' boys since the late 1930s. Menu favorites include all their sandwiches and the Fried chicken. On Saturday, they serve Dirty Rice a la carte or as a side with fried chicken. (Dirty rice gets its color and texture from the hearts, gizzards and livers that are chopped or minced and then reduced in a skillet before being baked with long grain rice.)

N7
1117 Montegut St, New Orleans, No phone
www.n7nola.com
CUISINE: French; some Japanese influences
DRINKS: Full bar
SERVING: Dinner; closed Sun
PRICE RANGE: $$
NEIGHBORHOOD: St. Claude / Bywater

Casual French restaurant, with the emphasis on casual. There's an old red Citroen out front in the lush garden, just to give you a reminder that we're "going French" tonight. You go in and sit at the copper-topped bar. The antiques were collected by the owners over the years. The focus is on seafood and small plates, including "can to table" items, as they have lots of fancy tinned foods—lobster rillettes from France, calamari in spicy ragout from Portugal. You get the can, a crisp baguette, put it together with some wine and you've got a fine little meal. Favorites: Sake cured salmon and Escargot tempura. Nice wine list. Courtyard dining available.

NAPOLEON HOUSE
500 Chartres St, New Orleans, 504-524-9752
www.napoleonhouse.com
CUISINE: American/Cafe
DRINKS: Full Bar
SERVING: Lunch, Dinner

PRICE RANGE: $$
NEIGHBORHOOD: French Quarter
This French Quarter historic landmark offers a Creole-Med menu with favorites like Muffalettas and Po' Boys. Now, you can get Muffuletta in any number of places in New Orleans, but it always made sense to me to eat it in a classic building that's over 200 years old. Adds a lot of atmosphere. You know what Muffaletta is, right? (It's ham, salami, pastrami, provolone and Swiss cheeses piled high on a round chewy loaf and topped with olive salad. What makes it special is that it's heated, not served cold.) If you're a fan of gin (as I am), try the classic Pimm's Cup; it's refreshing and rarely served in other places.

NOLA PO'BOYS
908 Bourbon St, New Orleans, 504-522-2639
No website
CUISINE: Seafood/Cajun/Creole
DRINKS: No Booze
SERVING: Lunch & Dinner
PRICE RANGE: $$
NEIGHBORHOOD: French Quarter
As the name states, this place sells Po'Boys and that's it. Great varieties like Fried catfish and Shrimp. Large portions.

PALM & PINE
308 N Rampart St., 504-814-6200
https://www.palmandpinenola.com/
CUISINE: Creole / Caribbean / Latin
DRINKS: Full Bar
SERVING: Dinner; Closed Tuesdays

PRICE RANGE: $$
NEIGHBORHOOD: French Quarter
Popular eatery located in an old French Quarter townhouse. They have a “tequila cart” that I am too wise to have them bring over because I know I’d get into trouble. Serves American fare with a Latin twist from a menu that changes seasonally. Favorites: Duck with mole; Apple Chorizo Chilaquiles; Boiled Peanut Salad (don’t ask); Fried Chicken Livers; Braised Duck Tamal; Goat Curry. Delicious desserts like Flan with caramelized bananas.

PARASOL’S
2533 Constance St, New Orleans, 504-354-9079
No Website
CUISINE: Cajun/Creole/American
DRINKS: Full bar
SERVING: Lunch & Dinner
PRICE RANGE: $
NEIGHBORHOOD: Irish Channel
Popular among locals but the lucky tourists find their way here for the great sandwiches. You can get a half-and-half (two different sandwiches in one). Try the shrimp and catfish or the grilled chicken with fries. Note: there’s a separate entrance is you’re just coming to eat.

PARKWAY BAKERY AND TAVERN
538 Hagan Ave, New Orleans, 504-482-3047
www.parkwaypoorboys.com
CUISINE: Seafood/Sandwiches
DRINKS: Full Bar
SERVING: Lunch & Dinner; closed Tues
PRICE RANGE: $$$
NEIGHBORHOOD: Bayou St. John
Popular neighborhood haunt known for its classic po'boys, and though they go back as far as 1911, they didn't start serving po'boys till 1929. Katrina put the place under 6 feet of water, but it wasn't long before they reopened and were serving their signature hot roast beef po'boys. Other super po'boys are created from alligator sausage links, BBQ beef or the hot dog po'boy. There's a surf n turf po'boy which has fried shrimp mixed with the roast beef and smothered in gravy. Sounds scary, huh? Order carefully because one sandwich is good for two. The bar attracts a lively local crowd, and it's always fun here. (And you cat eat there, thus avoiding the lines.)

PASCAL'S MANALE
1838 Napoleon Ave, New Orleans, 504-895-4877
www.pascalsmanale.com
CUISINE: Cajun/Creole
DRINKS: Full Bar
SERVING: Lunch, Dinner daily except Sunday when it's closed.
PRICE RANGE: $$$
NEIGHBORHOOD: Milan
The better oyster bars in New Orleans get their oysters from their own beds. This place is one example of that practice. This family owned eatery offers a menu of classic Cajun and Creole cuisine. Menu favorites include their Original BBQ Shrimp. Reservations recommended.

PECHE SEAFOOD GRILL
800 Magazine St, New Orleans, 504-522-1744
www.pecherestaurant.com
CUISINE: Seafood
DRINKS: Full Bar
SERVING: Lunch, Dinner
PRICE RANGE: $$$
NEIGHBORHOOD: Warehouse District
Here you'll find a menu of coastal seafood made with a modern twist to old world cooking. Many of the dishes are prepared on an open hearth over hardwood coals. Menu favorites include: Grab meat and fresh oysters. If you can tear yourself away from the lovely raw bar selections, go for the Gulf wahoo prepared 3 ways: the head that comes with salsa verde; the belly, served with a soy & chili glaze; and the collar, offered with a tart pepper jelly. I've never seen a dish like this elsewhere. The owners here wanted to veer

away from the typical fried seafood joints that proliferate in New Orleans. Maybe that's why the James Beard Foundation named it one of the Best New Restaurants in 2014.

PIECE OF MEAT
3301 Bienville St, New Orleans, 504-372-2289
https://www.pieceofmeatbutcher.com/
CUISINE: Butcher
DRINKS: Full Bar
SERVING: Lunch & Dinner, Closed Tues & Wed, Lunch only on Mon
PRICE RANGE: $$

NEIGHBORHOOD: Mid-City
Butcher shop offering a menu of sandwiches, charcuterie, and house-smoked ribs. Favorites: Turkey & Ham Sandwich and the "not turkey and the wolf bologna" sandwich. Vegetarian options. Outdoor seating, but nothing fancy.

PIZZA DELICIOUS
617 Piety St, New Orleans, 504-676-8482
www.pizzadelicious.com
CUISINE: Pizza/Italian
DRINKS: Beer & Wine Only
SERVING: Lunch & Dinner, closed Monday
PRICE RANGE: $$
NEIGHBORHOOD: Bywater
Casual counter-serve eatery serving thin-crust pizza. Small menu but usually crowded.

PYTHIAN MARKET
234 Loyola Ave, New Orleans, 504-481-9599
www.pythianmarket.com
CUISINE: Food Court
DRINKS: Full Bar
SERVING: 8 a.m. – 9 p.m.
PRICE RANGE: $$
NEIGHBORHOOD: Central Business District
In what was once the heart & soul of the African-American community, in 2018 the former Pythian "social club" was reimagined as a popular food court with eateries that emphasis local traditions. There's a pleasingly wide variety of choices, including everything from Brick-oven pizza, banh mi to Lobster Ceviche. Something for everyone.

R&O'S

216 Metairie-Hammond Hwy, Metairie, 504-831-1248

www.r-opizza.com

CUISINE: Pizza/Cajun/Creole

DRINKS: Full Bar

SERVING: Lunch daily, Dinner Wed - Sat

PRICE RANGE: $$

NEIGHBORHOOD: Metairie

A family restaurant that's usually packed and, trust me, it's because of the food, not the ambiance. Favorites include: hand tossed pizzas, Italian and seafood dishes, po'boys and their famous seafood gumbo. Still, if you only have time to visit this place once, get the roast beef po'boy. The beef is so tender. The gravy is rich and dark. The po'boy bread is toasted and the combination of these simple elements is wonderful. This place is a bit noisy and the TV is on for those wanting to watch the game.

R'EVOLUTION
777 Bienville St, New Orleans, 504-553-2277
www.revolutionnola.com/
CUISINE: Cajun/Creole
DRINKS: Full Bar
SERVING: Lunch, Dinner
PRICE RANGE: $$$$
NEIGHBORHOOD: French Quarter
This beautiful and luxurious restaurant offers an impressive menu of modern variations of Louisiana fare. The dishes showcase gulf fish, game and chops, salami, potted meats and terrines and pastas. Menu favorites include the Triptych of Quail with the birds

Southern-fried and stuffed with boudin sausage. Known for their delicious sweetbreads and one of the most extensive wine lists in town.

RALPH'S ON THE PARK
900 City Park Ave, New Orleans, 504-488-1000
www.ralphsonthepark.com/
CUISINE: Cajun/Creole
DRINKS: Full Bar
SERVING: Lunch & Dinner, Dinner only on Tues & Sat.
PRICE RANGE: $$$
NEIGHBORHOOD: City Park
Located in an old 1860's house, this upscale eatery offers a classic dining experience. Menu favorites include: fried eggs with red eye gravy, whole Gulf fish, mouthwatering items like lamb ragout with cream cheese grits or turtle soup with a liberal dash of sherry. Nice wine list. Popular Sunday brunch spot.

ROOK CAFÉ
4516 Freret St, New Orleans, 618-354-8114
http://therookcafe.com/
CUISINE: Cafe
DRINKS: No Booze
SERVING: Breakfast, Lunch & Dinner
PRICE RANGE: $
NEIGHBORHOOD: Freret

Relaxed café ideal for hanging with friends or just bring a book or your laptop. Nice selection of coffees, lattes, espressos and muffins.

SABA
5757 Magazine St, 504-324-7770
https://eatwithsaba.com/
CUISINE: Mediterranean / Middle Eastern / Israeli
DRINKS: Full Bar
SERVING: Lunch, & Dinner; Closed Mon & Tues.
PRICE RANGE: $$$
NEIGHBORHOOD: Uptown
Unpretentious but still trendy casual bistro atmosphere offering a menu of Middle Eastern fare. Small plates/family style dining. Favorites: Bulgarian Feta (with preserved leeks & coriander); Blue Crab Hummus; Squash wood-roasted; Moroccan Root Vegetables; Lamb Kebab. Popular neighborhood hangout.

Exterior at Saffron's

SAFFRON
4128 Magazine St, New Orleans, 504-323-2626
https://www.saffronnola.com/
CUISINE: Indian
DRINKS: Full Bar
SERVING: Dinner, Closed Sun & Mon
PRICE RANGE: $$$
NEIGHBORHOOD: Downtown
Upscale eatery with a flattering lighting plan that makes everybody look good offering Indian cuisine with a New Orleans flair. They mix up not only local cuisines (Creole & Cajun) but also mix up Northern and Southern Indian dishes. The results are truly something different, something you don't see

anywhere else in the U.S. My Favorites: Goat Masala; a Gumbo that mixes Indian with Creole cuisine; and Bombay Shrimp (in fact, any shrimp dish you get here will be special). I always get the Paneer Pudha, which is a pancake made with lentils served with date and mint chutneys. It's bursting with flavor. You must try the Ginger Crème Brûlée. Craft cocktails.

SAINT-GERMAIN
3054 St. Claude Ave, 504-218-8729
https://saintgermainnola.com/
CUISINE: French
DRINKS: Wine
SERVING: Dinner, Lunch on Sat & Sun; Closed Wednesdays
PRICE RANGE: $$
NEIGHBORHOOD: Bywater
In a funky little cottage you'll find this Paris-style wine bar (with an excellent selection of wines by the glass) that has a separate though adjacent (reservation only) dining room. Don't let the neon sign outside that reads "Sugar Park" Pizza" fool you. House made cheese and chicken liver. Menu changes daily, but whatever they serve the night you go will be superior. (Be sure to opt in for the wine pairing deal they will offer you.) The freshly baked bread will blow you away. Reservations necessary.

SAMMY'S
3000 Elysian Fields Ave, New Orleans, 504-947-0675
www.sammysfood.com
CUISINE: Peruvian

DRINKS: No Booze
SERVING: Breakfast, Lunch & Dinner; closed Sun
PRICE RANGE: $$
NEIGHBORHOOD: St. Roch
There's usually a line at the counter. Great Po'Boys and other favorites like Seafood eggplant. They have

a great fried trout po'boy distinctive for its crispy cornmeal crust. Large portions. Poker machines.

SATSUMA CAFE
7901 Maple St, New Orleans, 504-309-5557
www.satsumacafe.com
CUISINE: Bakery/Cafe
DRINKS: No Booze
SERVING: Breakfast, Lunch
PRICE RANGE: $$
NEIGHBORHOOD: Uptown, Black Pearl
This is a bakery with a great menu of sandwiches, subs, gluten-free and vegan items. Here you'll find an interesting selection of fresh juices, like the tart and sweet Popeye juice. This is a very popular lunch spot that always crowded. Excellent coffee & cappuccino.

SEAWORTHY
ACE HOTEL
630 Carondelet St, 504-930-3071
http://www.seaworthynola.com/
https://www.acehotel.com/neworleans/
CUISINE: Seafood
DRINKS: Full Bar
SERVING: Dinner, Lunch on Sat & Sun.
PRICE RANGE: $$
NEIGHBORHOOD: Old Naples
Quaint eatery opened by the Ace Hotel in an old cottage from the 1830s. You'd never know the Ace had anything to do with this place, it's so completely different. Offering an impressive menu of locally sourced oysters and seafood. Has a great long bar where it's fun to sample some of their always-changing selection of oysters and drink some wine. I put away 3 dozen at one sitting accompanied by a very nice white burgundy. The wide-planked floor and high dark doors and wood trimming give you the feeling you're in New England or a Dublin pub, especially when it's raining outside. There are some tables out back in a kind of alleyway where you sit under towering brick walls that belong to adjacent buildings. Favorites: Grilled octopus; Swordfish with sunchokes; Anchovy Toast; Coconut & pineapple gulf fish ceviche. Wine pairings.

SHAYA
4213 Magazine St, New Orleans, 504-891-4213
www.shayarestaurant.com
CUISINE: Middle Eastern/Mediterranean

DRINKS: Full bar
SERVING: Lunch & Dinner
PRICE RANGE: $$
NEIGHBORHOOD: Touro
Casual restaurant offering a menu of modern Israeli fare. The pita bread that comes from the oven is soft as a baby's pillow and the smell fills the room with a comforting aroma. Favorites: Crispy Halloumi (Peaches, Smoked Turkish Chilies, and Pecans) and Lamb Shank. Back patio.

SOBOU
310 Chartres Street, New Orleans, 504-552-4095
www.sobounola.com
CUISINE: Cajun/Creole
DRINKS: Full Bar
SERVING: Breakfast, Lunch, Dinner
PRICE RANGE: $$

NEIGHBORHOOD: French Quarter
Sobou offers a menu of comfort food with a modern twist. Menu favorites include: Crispy Oyster Taco and Crispy Chicken on the Bone. For a treat, try the Foie Gras Float or the Cherries Jubilee & White Chocolate Bread Pudding.

ST. JAMES CHEESE CO.
5004 Prytania St, New Orleans, 504-899-4737
www.stjamescheese.com
CUISINE: Cheese Shop / Sandwiches
DRINKS: Beer & Wine Only
SERVING: Lunch & Dinner
PRICE RANGE: $$
NEIGHBORHOOD: Uptown
This tiny combination sandwich shop and market offers a great selection of cheeses. The charcuterie boards are among the best in town. The crowd is trendy and fun. In good weather, try to get a seat under the shade trees in the courtyard.

SYLVAIN
625 Chartres St, New Orleans, 504-265-8123
www.sylvainnola.com
CUISINE: American/Gastropub
DRINKS: Full Bar
SERVING: Dinner
PRICE RANGE: $$
NEIGHBORHOOD: French Quarter
This small gastropub offers an inventive menu with a strong bar serving delicious creative cocktails, like the Gunshop Fizz, made with rum and ginger beer they make here on the premises. A favorite of hipsters

and foodies (and hip younger locals, who normally don't go into the French Quarter), it's also offers a nice courtyard for dining. Chef Alex Harrell offers up menu favorites like Braised Beef Cheeks, Prochetta Po'Boys and Roasted Texas Quail as well as excellent daily specials.

TABLEAU
616 St Peter St, New Orleans, 504-934-3463
www.tableaufrenchquarter.com
CUISINE: Cajun/Creole
DRINKS: Full Bar
SERVING: Lunch, Dinner
PRICE RANGE: $$$
NEIGHBORHOOD: French Quarter
Located on Jackson Square at Le Petit Theatre, this is Dickie Brennan's newest restaurant. Chef Ben Thibodeaus offers a menu showcasing regional

ingredients and classic French Creole cuisine. Menu favorites include Fried Eggplant Batons and Filet of Beef Bearnaise. There's an open kitchen in the main dining room so the guests can see the chef at work. This is a three-story restaurant with several private dining rooms and courtyard seating. Open daily with brunch served on the weekends.

TOUPS MEATERY
845 N Carrollton Ave, New Orleans, 504-252-4999
www.toupsmeatery.com
CUISINE: Cajun/Creole
DRINKS: Full Bar
SERVING: Lunch, Dinner
PRICE RANGE: $$
NEIGHBORHOOD: Mid-City
Chef Isaac Toups offers a contemporary Cajun menu inspired by deep-rooted Louisiana family traditions. Here the food is excellent with menu favorites like: Pork Chops and Short Ribs. Dessert lovers should

save room for the Doberge cake, a multi-layered sugary confection available in several flavors.

TURKEY AND THE WOLF
739 Jackson Ave, New Orleans, 504-218-7428
www.turkeyandthewolf.com
CUISINE: Sandwiches/Desserts
DRINKS: Full bar
SERVING: Lunch & Dinner; closed Tues
PRICE RANGE: $$
NEIGHBORHOOD: Lower Garden District
Funky no-frills sandwich shop with retro tables from the 1950s, weird salt shakers, etc. Menu features an inventive list of sandwiches and cocktails. Favorites: Chicken pot pie and Lamb neck roti (with cucumber and onions). The chef here is gourmet-trained, but likes things on the casual side. Very high quality food is served here.

VERTI MARTE
1201 Royal St, New Orleans, 504-525-4767
No Website
CUISINE: Sandwiches/Salad
DRINKS: Beer & Wine
SERVING: Open 24 hours
PRICE RANGE: $
NEIGHBORHOOD: French Quarter
Market and deli known for decades for its Creole inspired sandwiches. Popular stop for those out drinking all night. Favorite: Jazz po'boy made with a heaping pile of roast turkey, ham, American and Swiss cheese, sautéed mushrooms, tomatoes, Cajun

seasoned grilled shrimp and their "special" sauce. The muffuletta here (served hot or cold) has more meat than beard, which is really good.

WAYNE JACOB'S SMOKEHOUSE
769 West 5th St, LaPlace, 985-652-9990
https://wjsmokehouse.com/
CUISINE: Smokehouse
DRINKS: Full Bar
SERVING: Lunch, Dinner, Brunch
PRICE RANGE: $$
NEIGHBORHOOD: LaPlace
A bit out of the way in LaPlace, but worth the trip. Favorites: Pork Snack Sticks; Fresh Deer Sausage; Whole Smoked Chicken; Pork Loin stuffed with andouille; Smoked Sausage Philly and Spaghetti and Meatballs. Doughnut bread pudding is a must. Popular for Brunch (menu changes weekly). The Bloody Mary here is very nice.

The line at Willie Mae's

WILLIE MAE'S SCOTCH HOUSE
2401 St Ann St, New Orleans, 504-822-9503
www.williemaesnola.com/
CUISINE: Southern, Comfort Food
DRINKS: No Booze
SERVING: Breakfast, Lunch
PRICE RANGE: $$
NEIGHBORHOOD: Mid-City, Treme
Willie Mae's is known for its delicious comfort food like their America's Best Fried Chicken. The only drawback is that it's a bit out of the way. Closed Sundays.

YE OLDE COLLEGE INN
3000 S Carrollton Ave, New Orleans, 504-866-3683
www.collegeinn1933.com
CUISINE: Southern/Creole/Cajun/American
DRINKS: Full bar
SERVING: Dinner; closed Sun & Mon
PRICE RANGE: $$
NEIGHBORHOOD: Gert Town
Casual eatery with a nice menu of Southern-Creole comfort food. Favorites Crawfish and Seafood gumbo. You must try their fried bread pudding for dessert.

NIGHTLIFE

WWOZ 90.7 FM
www.wwoz.org
Tune in to this radio station when you first get to town. It plays a lot of jazz & blues, but it's completely dedicated to the local music scene. A good way to find out what's going on. This will certainly get you in the right mood to party in New Orleans.

3 KEYS
THREE KEYS
ACE HOTEL
600 Carondelet St, 504-900-1180

http://threekeysnola.com/
https://www.acehotel.com/neworleans/
NEIGHBORHOOD: Downtown
Intimate venue (maybe 50 seats) offering live music. Hosts lots of free shows. Cocktails and music.

ALTO
ACE HOTEL
600 Carondelet St, 504-900-1180
https://www.acehotel.com/neworleans/
NEIGHBORHOOD: Downtown
Rooftop garden and bar. Menu of Italian salads and small plates. Cocktails, craft beer and wine. Unbelievable views of downtown. Enjoy cocktails poolside.

BAR MARILOU
MAISON DE LA LUZ
544 Carondelet St, 504-814-7711
https://www.barmarilou.com/
NEIGHBORHOOD: Business and arts district
Delicious creative cocktails and a small menu. Be sure to explore the lobby of this gorgeously reimagined hotel property just dripping with Southern charm. You'll wish you stayed here instead of wherever it is you're staying.

BAR TONIQUE
820 N Rampart St, New Orleans, 504-324-6045
www.bartonique.com
Popular among locals and visitors, this neighborhood bar mixes up classic cocktails with fresh ingredients. Great place to stop for a cocktail before dinner.

BJ'S LOUNGE
4301 Burgundy St, New Orleans, 504-945-9256
No Website
NEIGHBORHOOD: Bywater
If you like crowded smoke filled dive bars, this is your place. It's usually packed with locals who know each other. There's live music on Monday nights featuring bands like King James and the Special Men. Free red beans & rice on Mondays. Pool tables. Cash only.

BUD RIP'S
900 Piety St, New Orleans, 504-945-5762
No Website
NEIGHBORHOOD: Bywater
This is just a classic neighborhood bar with TVs being the only frills. Some call it a dive bar, but they still show up for happy hour. There is also a pool table, dartboard and video poker. Smoking allowed.

CANDLELIGHT LOUNGE
925 North Robertson St, New Orleans, 504-957-4459
No Website
NEIGHBORHOOD: Treme
This popular Jazz & Blues Club happens to be a favorite stop for the secodline parades and the Treme Brass Band makes a stop here every Wednesday night and takes the stage. Cheap drinks and very friendly crowd. Cover on Wednesday nights.

CAROUSEL PIANO BAR & LOUNGE
Hotel Monteleone
214 Rue Royal, New Orleans, 504-523-3341
www.hotelmonteleone.com/new-orleans-dining-entertainment/carousel-bar-lounge/
NEIGHBORHOOD: French Quarter
Here you can enjoy live jazz, blues, a mint julep, and people watch without moving as it's the only revolving bar in New Orleans. Located in the **Hotel Monteleone** overlooking Royal Street. This is a long-time favorite of locals and tourists who love to sit at the 24-seat revolving carousel bar. They've expanded the place so now there's a split-level viewing area as well as street level views.

CURE
4905 Freret St, New Orleans, 504-302-2357
www.curenola.com
NEIGHBORHOOD: Freret, Uptown
This is an unpretentious (although very hip) cocktail bar located in a repurposed firehouse on a dark corner that offers a creative menu of bar snacks. Not just a place to drink, but also a place to relax and enjoy the experience. Great selection of cocktails that have been designed by serious mixologists with a strong emphasis on the house-made bitters. The cocktail menu changes 8 times a year. Bar menu features items like Steak Tartare, Jamaican meat pies, baked crabcakes and Maitake Mushrooms. This was probably New Orleans's first craft cocktail bar, but there are numerous others ones now.

D.B.A.
618 Frenchman, New Orleans, 504-942-3731
www.dbaneworleans.com
NEIGHBORHOOD: Marigny
This live music club offers a roster of local and regional acts. The bar serves beer, wine and spirits in a smoke-free environment. Cover charge.

ELYSIAN BAR
HOTEL PETER & PAUL
2317 Burgundy St, 504-356-6769
https://www.theelysianbar.com/
NEIGHBORHOOD: Faubourg Marigny District
Chic hotel bar in what was an old rectory where they put a lot of work into the décor—gingham, rattan

furniture, glittering sconces, all coming together to throw off a very 19th Century atmosphere. Has a very nice food menu, from the Grilled Okra and Crispy Eggplant to the Crispy Beef Cheeks and a Duck Egg Omelette that really hits the spot. Creative and classic cocktails. Charming atmosphere, even out in the aged-brick courtyard where you sit beneath the old stained-glass windows from the church.

FRENCH 75 BAR
813 Bienville St, New Orleans, 504-523-5433
www.arnaudsrestaurant.com/french-75
NEIGHBORHOOD: French Quarter
This is a very popular New Orleans bar but it also gets pretty smoky. The drinks are top notch and the crowd is interesting as this is a side bar to Arnaud's, one of the great dining spots of the French Quarter. Try their Herbsaint Frappe, which might be called the

mojito for New Orleans, but flavored with anise liqueur.

HI-HO LOUNGE
2239 St Claude Ave, 504-945-4446
www.hiholounge.net
NEIGHBORHOOD: St Roch
This neighborhood bar is also a live music venue that has been one of the pioneers in the underground alternative music scene. The variety of music includes indie rock, hip hop, electronic, jazz, funk and jam music. Other entertainment offered includes burlesque performances, comedy acts, and film screenings. No smoking allowed. Daily food specials offered and a guy cooks BBQ out front.

JEAN LAFITTE'S OLD ABSINTHE HOUSE
240 Bourbon St, New Orleans, 504-523-4640
www.ruebourbon.com
NEIGHBORHOOD: French Quarter
Built in 1807 as a corner grocery, this landmark saloon has become a must-see destination for locals and tourists. Unique round bar seating. Large cocktail selection. No food but they have free popcorn and an inexpensive juke box.

LATITUDE 29
BIENVILLE HOUSE
321 N Peters St, New Orleans, 504-609-3811
www.latitude29nola.com
NEIGHBORHOOD: French Quarter
A Tiki-style gastropub with a great bar menu of exotic cocktails located in the Bienville House which

dates back to the 1830s. Locals' hangout. There's a lovely courtyard with a pool. A place to get away from the noise and mayhem one usually finds in the French Quarter. Ask about the great cocktails not on the menu.

LOA
221 Camp St, New Orleans, 504-553-9550
www.ihhotel.com
Located in: International House
Popular New Orleans watering hole frequented by local artists, business owners and tourists. Located in the International House Hotel, this bar serves up a great selection of handcrafted cocktails, classics, and made to order concoctions.

Maple Leaf

MAPLE LEAF BAR
8316 Oak St, New Orleans, 504-866-9359
www.mapleleafbar.com
NEIGHBORHOOD: Uptown
This is dive live music venue is one of the longest operating music clubs in New Orleans. Live music 7 nights a week and they feature every music genre including blues, funk, R&B, rock, zydeco, jazz and jam bands with a schedule that includes local performers and touring national acts.

MARKEY'S BAR
640 Louisa St, New Orleans, 504-943-0785
www.markeysbar.com
NEIGHBORHOOD: Bywater
This friendly neighborhood bar specializes in beer on tap and good bar food. This is a local hangout for watching the game serving up about 15 beers on tap. There are 8 TVs that play a variety of sports games.

MIMI'S IN THE MARIGNY
2600 Chartres St, New Orleans, 504-872-9868
www.mimismarigny.com
NEIGHBORHOOD: Marigny
The DJ here plays a lot of old New Orleans "swamp music." There's a soul funk dance party on Saturday night.

OAK
8118 Oak St, New Orleans, 504-302-1485
www.oaknola.com
NEIGHBORHOOD: Uptown
This place offers an impressive selection of wines with nearly a hundred hand-selected bottles. The

bartenders serve some great signature cocktails. Live music consists of jazz, acoustic folk or R&B. Full menu available.

PIRATE'S ALLEY

622 Pirates Alley, New Orleans, 504-524-9332
www.piratesalleycafe.com
NEIGHBORHOOD: French Quarter
Cozy little bar that opens very early (for those that need a rum before 10 a.m.) Serving great cocktails including Absinthe, served the traditional way with the absinthe water fountain, sugar cube and slotted spoon. Cash only.

ROCK 'N' BOWL

3016 S Carrollton Ave, New Orleans, 504-861-1700
www.rocknbowl.com
CUISINE: Bowling
DRINKS: Full bar
SERVING: Lunch & Dinner; closed Sun
PRICE RANGE: $$$
NEIGHBORHOOD: Gert Town
Bowling alley, bar, and stage for live music. Great selection of music. Menu is typical bar grub.

SAINTS & SINNERS
627 Bourbon St, New Orleans, 504-528-9307
http://saintsandsinnersnola.com
NEIGHBORHOOD: French Quarter
Channing Tatum's trendy two-level lounge with an old-time bordello feel. Don't expect to see Mr. Channing, even though it's usually filled with ladies hoping he'll make an appearance. Live DJ. Nice bar grub menu featuring favorites like Alligator tacos and gumbo fries.

SNAKE AND JAKE'S CHRISTMAS CLUB LOUNGE
7612 Oak St, New Orleans, 504-861-2802
www.snakeandjakes.com
NEIGHBORHOOD: Uptown
This is a small, neighborhood bar that great for late nights. It's been voted "New Orleans Best Dive Bar" many times and has a loyal following. Music provide by the jukebox. Smoking allowed.

SPOTTED CAT MUSIC CLUB
623 Frenchman, New Orleans, 504-943-3887
www.spottedcatmusicclub.com
NEIGHBORHOOD: Marigny

This live jazz bar is a favorite among the locals. The performers often ask people onstage to dance but there's also a small dance floor.

ST. ROCH TAVERN
1200 St Roch Ave, New Orleans, 504-945-0194
No Website
NEIGHBORHOOD: St Roch
This popular dive has a welcoming neighborhood feel with cheap drinks and a tasty bar menu. On Saturday nights there's a punk rock dance party that's become legendary. It's been called the sweatiest sissy bounce party in town. Cash only.

THE SWAMP
516 Bourbon St, New Orleans, 504-231-8519
www.bourbon-swamp.com
NEIGHBORHOOD: French Quarter
Popular nightspot with a gator theme and neon lights that features a mechanical bull in the courtyard. Wrap-around balcony typical of New Orleans. Upstairs, downstairs and outdoor patio filled with a young, attractive crowd. Offers great deals like 3 for 1 beers. Try the Swamp Juice – a giant cocktail of questionable ingredients, but it packs a punch.

THREE MUSES
536 Frenchmen St, New Orleans, 504-252-4801
www.3musesnola.com/
NEIGHBORHOOD: Marigny
This relaxed nightspot offers a great mix of music and cocktails. It's a locals' hangout and is usually crowded. This is another haunt for those who like specialty cocktails, like the Spaghetti Western (bourbon, orange Campari & rosemary syrup). If you want a table, be prepared to wait. Food available. No smoking.

TWELVE MILE LIMIT
500 S Telemachus St, New Orleans, 504-488-8114
www.twelvemilelimit.com
NEIGHBORHOOD: Mid-City
What other bar offers a haircut and a cocktail for $10 (Sundays only)? This unusual nightspot offers free food on Mondays and there's a live dating show on the last Thursday of the month. This dog-friendly bar features a pool table, craft cocktails, a menu heavily tilted toward BBQ and gourmet desserts (like the excellent doberge cake). The Great Idea cocktail is a mixture of vodka, amara and ginger beer. Smoking on the patio.

VITASCOPE HALL
601 Loyola Ave, New Orleans, 504-561-1234
www.neworleans.hyatt.com/en/hotel/dining/VitascopeHall.html
NEIGHBORHOOD: French Quarter
Named after the world's first for-profit movie theater in New Orleans, this place features 42 flat screen TVs and its own iPhone and Android application to keep guests up to date. One of the best bars in New Orleans with quite an active nightlife scene. Specialty cocktails stand out here, like the Praline Sling, their version of the Sazerac, made with bourbon, pecan bitters, absinthe and caramel.

INDEX

N

O

P

R

S

T

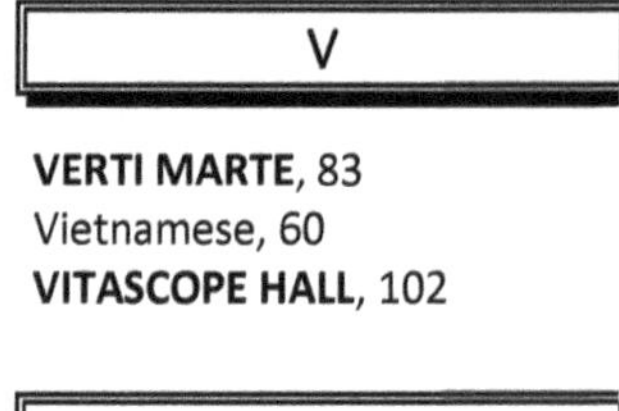

V

W

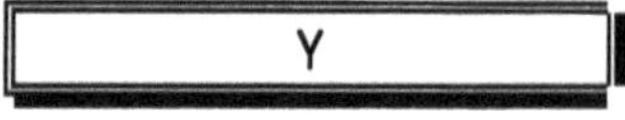

Y

www.ingramcontent.com/pod-product-compliance
Ingram Content Group UK Ltd.
Pitfield, Milton Keynes, MK11 3LW, UK
UKHW021647190726
13853UKWH00001B/115

9 798201 732530